IMAGES OF ENGLAND

UPMINSTER AND HORNCHURCH

IMAGES OF ENGLAND

UPMINSTER AND HORNCHURCH

TONY BENTON

TEMPUS

Frontispiece: Upminster Peace celebrations, 1919. The slogan 'The food that builds bonnie babies' was first introduced by Glaxo to promote their skimmed milk and baby products in 1913 and was clearly a well-known catchphrase by the time this Upminster resident chose his humorous outfit to take part in the celebrations for the end of the war. The company was actually founded in New Zealand in 1873 by London-born Joseph Edward Nathan.

First published 2004

Tempus Publishing Limited
The Mill, Brimscombe Port,
Stroud, Gloucestershire, GL5 2QG
www.tempus-publishing.com

© Tony Benton, 2004

The right of Tony Benton to be identified as the Author
of this work has been asserted in accordance with the
Copyrights, Designs and Patents Act 1988.

British Library Cataloguing in Publication Data.
A catalogue record for this book is available from the British Library.

ISBN 0 7524 3206 0

Typesetting and origination by Tempus Publishing Limited.
Printed in Great Britain by Midway Colour Print, Wiltshire.

Contents

Acknowledgements

I would again like to thank all those who have helped over the past ten years or so that I have been gathering information on Upminster and Hornchurch. In addition I would like to thank Tony Fox for his interest, help, kind words and encouragement over the past few years.

The illustrations in this edition are all from my own collection of postcards and photographs, with the exceptions noted below. All reasonable steps have been taken to trace copyright owners and I am grateful to the following people for allowing me to copy and reproduce photographs and illustrations from their collections: Joan Hills – pages 55, 56 (bottom) and 62; Chris Saltmarsh – pages 63 (top), 95 and 97; June Muncey – page 15 (bottom); Don Bradnam – page 32; Mary Killingback – page 34; Jack Clippingdale – page 37 (top); Mrs B. Gooden – page 68 (bottom); and F.G. 'Dicky' Bird – page 122 (bottom).

Introduction

As a local builder, and much more, Thomas Lewis Wilson (1833-1919) was well placed to observe the changes taking place in the pretty Essex village of Upminster where he was born, lived, worked and eventually died.

When Wilson's *Sketches of Upminster* was published in 1856 his home village was in every way the 'small rural parish' he lovingly described. Many of the great houses of the parish were less than a hundred years old, and Upminster's notable windmill was little more than fifty years old. Two schools had recently been built for the parish children, but as Wilson noted there was 'neither a mechanics' institute nor reading room'. Within a few years the parish church had been extensively remodelled, but little else of significance had changed by 1881 when Wilson's updated volume *History and Topography of Upminster* appeared, although this enlarged volume benefited from the earliest photographs of the parish and specially commissioned engravings.

Wilson was close at hand when the first turf was ceremonially cut on an Upminster hilltop in October 1883 marking the start of the railway extension from Barking to Pitsea, which in 1885 brought Upminster its direct rail connection to London. By 1893 Upminster's transport network was further extended with rail links to Romford and Grays. Although the expected development of the parish was still almost twenty years away, modernisation was unavoidable as Upminster's first parish council was elected in 1894, with T.L. Wilson one of the nine councillors. The local water supply, drawn mainly from abundant local springs, was supplemented with mains water, while the village and the outlying hamlet of Corbets Tey were connected to mains sewage in 1898.

The first housing developments in Upminster, which had started by 1904 on the Branfill Park estate (Gaynes, Branfill and Champion Roads), were just a flavour of the major redevelopment that followed from late 1906. The Upminster Garden Suburb was developed by W.P. Griggs & Co. and their successors Upminster Estates Ltd on lands which were part of the Upminster Hall estate. The detached and large semi-detached houses around Hall Lane changed not only the physical face of Upminster but also the social structure, attracting new, mainly middle-class, inhabitants. It was followed by further well-planned housing development on the former Gaynes Park estate after 1930 and other smaller estates in the south of the parish. As a result Upminster's population grew from 1,477 in 1901 to 5,732 in 1931 and an estimated 11,000 in 1941.

With no industry of its own, Upminster's people mainly owed their living to local farms or small trades. The new population of the twentieth century typically commuted to London to work, or worked in industries nearby, such as Dagenham's Ford Motor Company, many of whose executives settled in Upminster.

Despite sharing a common boundary along the River Ingrebourne, the neighbouring communities of Upminster and Hornchurch have long retained separate characters. Although only a few miles nearer to London, Hornchurch seems to have been less isolated and, although its economy was mainly rural, it was also strongly influenced by industrial concerns operating in the village centre from the late eighteenth century. The Hornchurch brewery supplied inns and beerhouses for miles around, employing sixty staff at its peak around 1900, while Wedlake's innovative Fairkytes iron foundry had even wider influence, achieving regional and national renown for its cast-iron agricultural implements after its foundation by Thomas and Robert Wedlake around 1809. A smaller industry developed from the wheelwright's trade in the late nineteenth century as Charles Frost branched out from making carriages and other wheeled vehicles into building motor vehicle bodies in the early 1900s at new premises in North Street.

Hornchurch is also fortunate in having a local historian who recorded much of the parish history. But Hornchurch's recorder, Charles Thomas Perfect (1864-1939), was not a local man, as he hailed from Surrey, only coming to Hornchurch in around 1902 and returning to his native county in 1928. By the time of Perfect's arrival in Hornchurch, the development of the parish was well under way, although the village centre retained its seventeenth-century feel, with many older buildings surviving. The earliest residential building in the parish started in the 1860s when the development of neighbouring Romford spread across the boundary into north-west Hornchurch, and this continued over the next few decades south of Brentwood Road.

The development of the Emerson Park estate on the southern part of the manor of Nelmes by William Carter from 1895 was the first significant development close to Hornchurch village, followed within a decade by Alfred Barber's development of the adjacent Great Nelmes estate; both comprised large houses on spacious plots. Before 1900 other smaller properties were developed closer to the village centre, more suitable for the working population.

The suburban development of Hornchurch gathered pace after 1920 as numerous farms and estates were put up for sale. This rapid expansion continued in the 1930s, including the major Elm Park estate, which was developed by Richard Costain Ltd from January 1934. The Hornchurch Urban District Council (UDC) was founded in 1926, and expanded in 1934 to include Upminster, Cranham, Rainham, Wennington and parts of Great Warley and North Ockendon. Private- and public-sector house-building continued in the post-war period and by 1956, with a population of 110,000, Hornchurch was the second-largest UDC in England.

This book features some of Hornchurch's military connections. Grey Towers Mansion was requisitioned for war service in 1914; it became the camp for the Sportsman's Battalion of the Royal Fusiliers in 1914-15 and then the convalescent hospital of the New Zealand contingent between 1916 and 1919. Suttons Farm airfield opened in 1915 as part of London's air defences and gained fame the next year when Lt William Leefe Robinson, who was based there, was awarded the Victoria Cross for his exploits in becoming the first airman to shoot down a German airship. During the Second World War the airfield, by now known as RAF Hornchurch, was famous for its part in the Battle of Britain.

Upminster and Hornchurch's rapid growth coincided with the golden age of postcards, which flourished in the Edwardian period and continued to be popular through the inter-war years. Not surprisingly postcards provide a rich source for the images in this book, complemented by family collections and other sources.

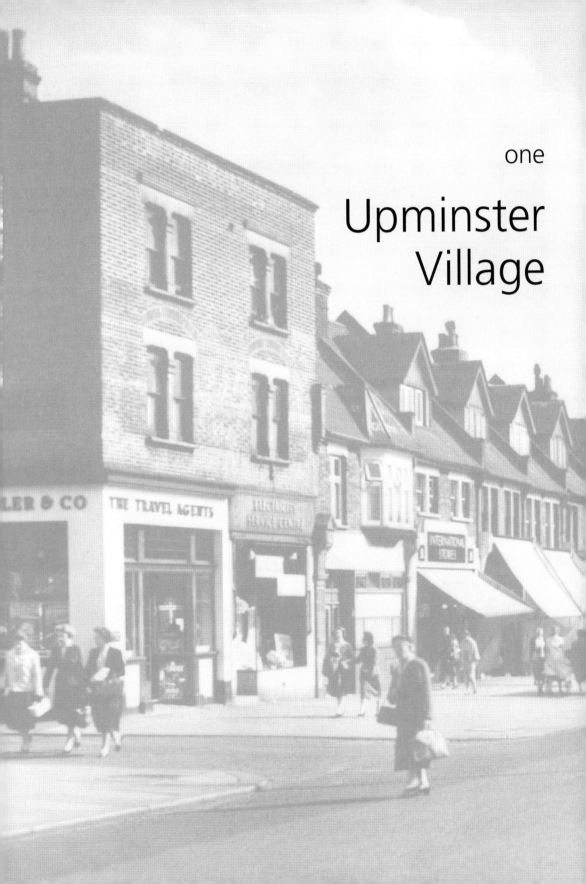

one

Upminster
Village

A van from the Albany Laundry, Tilbury, stands outside the Bell Hotel in 1908, while Eldred's smithy alongside seems to be in demand. The Bell was one of many local buildings developed by Sir James Esdaile from 1760 when he became lord of the manor of Gaynes.

A fine summer day around 1930 and the Bell sports a new entrance. Watney, who took over the London and Burton Brewery of Stepney in 1929 now supplies the beer. The landmark large chestnut tree gave its name to the adjacent house and to Aggiss' Chestnuts Garage, which lay behind it.

By the mid-1930s the four-way signpost at Bell Corner has given way to a traffic island pointing down Corbets Tey Road as the modern era approaches. Within a few years the scene was to be further transformed: the tree and houses were taken down in late 1937 to make way for Burton's men's clothing store.

The Cosy Corner around 1910, a few years after Arthur Burgess, a Romford tobacconist, had bought the premises from the Rowe family. It was built by William Hammond around 1831 and was often known as the 'old butcher's shop' after its original use. Rowe had run a grocer's and draper's store there but Burgess developed the Cosy Corner as a popular confectioner's.

Above: Sidney Abraham stands outside his baker's shop in Station Road, probably with his son Sidney, who died in Germany as a prisoner of war in 1918, and his youngest daughter Rosie. Another son Albert (Bert) Abraham took over the business in 1932 on Sidney's death but under the terms of his grandfather Edward Hitch's will it had to be sold when his mother Florence died. Hornchurch District Council bought the premises at auction in March 1952 and Bert received notice to quit. Bert knew no other trade and, unable to find work, in July 1952 he drowned in a South Ockendon sandpit; the inquest returned a verdict that he took his life.

Opposite above: Looking northwards up the recently built Station Road on a grey day in 1910. A small group of smocked children stand in front of Talbot's wheelwright's shop, later Talbot's garage. This was demolished in late 2000 and replaced by the Roomes furniture store.

Opposite below: John and Lily Caldecourt sit surrounded by their nine children in around 1910. The two tallest boys are Albion and Frederick, who lost their lives in the First World War. Standing between them is Sidney, with Ernie on the right of the photograph. Also standing (left to right) are Elsie, Maud and Lily, with Daisy, Edward (Ted) and Annie in front. John opened his plumbing and glazing business on Station Road (later No.22) in around 1899, taking over the premises owned by William Hook, builder. After John's death in 1926 Ernie continued the business, with Ted trading as a decorator from the same premises.

The parade of shops in Station Road on an overcast morning in 1917. In the centre of the parade the lamps mark Searson's boot and shoe shop, which opened in April 1908 and remained in business until the late 1980s. By the 1930s the white-fronted shop next door, here named Tom Brown's, was Rumsey's fish shop. Next is Harry Talbot, greengrocer's, and on the right is Miss Rhoda Leany's confectioner's shop.

The same Station Road parade in about 1927. On the opposite side of the road the first Roomes Store has not yet been built but beyond is the Westminster Bank, built in 1911; it was later replaced by an extension of Roomes. Roomes also acquired Dr Bletsoe's house, on the other corner of Branfill Road, on the doctor's retirement in 1939.

Right: Ernest Rose Holden Gates started business in Hornchurch in partnership with John Read, striking out in his own right when he opened his premises at 40 Station Road in 1921. His son Ernest Bridger 'Tiny' Gates joined him in 1926, and after E.R.H. Gates' retirement through ill health in 1929 he was in charge until he too stepped down in 1935, partly through ill-health. Hubert Cardnell, Robert Langdon, David Williams and Albert Parish became directors of the new company, Gates & Son Ltd, which became Gates Parish & Co. in 1945 when Albert Parish took control.

Below: The Bonanza at No.7 Broadway (now 42 Station Road) was bought for Gladys Bolton by her parents in 1920, a year after she married Sidney Bolton. The Bonanza sold toys, knitwear, drapery and much more besides. Gladys ran it with the help of Daisy Cudby, and later Ivy Wakefield, until the business was sold in 1939.

Above: Chandler & Company Travel Agents originally operated from the owner Harry Chandler's home in Springfield Court but by the early 1950s opened their business in half of the corner shop, later acquiring the adjacent electric board shop. It is now a nationally renowned company.

Opposite above: The dustbins and other ironware on the pavement on the right confirm that the first Roomes store (built 1927) has recently opened. On the left, Percy Goodchild's milliner's and draper's occupies the ground floor of the large building on the corner of Howard Road, and Copley's ironmonger's can be seen next door.

Opposite below: Upminster's Congregational Church opened on the corner of Gaynes Road on 29 March 1911, six years before this photograph was taken. It was built at a cost of around £4,000, raised by donation and subscription, replacing the former chapel on Upminster Hill which was sold to the Plymouth Brethren for £400.

Upminster station opened for business on 1 May 1885 connecting Upminster with rail services to the London, Tilbury & Southend Railway's Fenchurch Street terminus, as part of the Barking–Pitsea extension. The main entrance was moved onto Hall Lane when the station was remodelled in 1931, but this side entrance reopened a few years ago.

Upminster's rail connections were extended in 1891 with the addition of a single-track link to Grays, and two years later with the addition of a route to Romford, via Emerson Park. The station buildings at Upminster included a subway connecting the main up and down platforms.

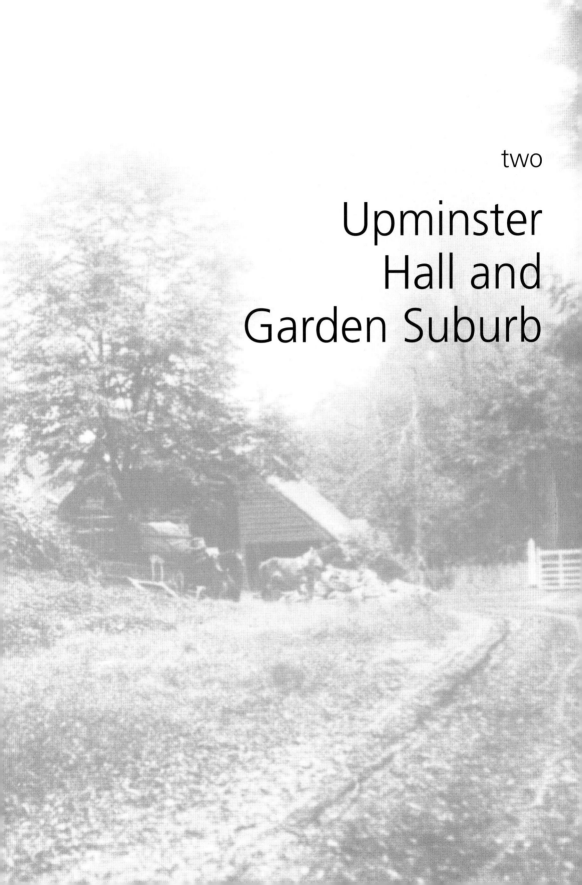

two

Upminster Hall and Garden Suburb

Above: Looking north across the Hall Lane railway bridge on a summer evening around 1900. Within a few years this scene was to be transformed as W.P. Griggs developed the Upminster Garden Suburb on land bought from the Upminster Hall estate in 1906. Building began the following year.

Opposite above: An early photograph of Upminster Hall, around 1900. The Hall and large adjoining estate was the home of the Branfill family for two centuries after its purchase in 1685 by Captain Andrew Branfill for £7,400. Parts of the timber-framed hall probably date to the late fifteenth century.

Opposite below: A rare photograph of the interior of Upminster Hall, showing the oldest part of the house around 1900. Many fine paintings of family members adorned the walls of the hall, dining room and drawing room. The Hall became the club house of Upminster Golf Club in 1927.

A rural scene close to Upminster Hall in about 1906. The nearby thatched Tithe Barn, which now houses a fine collection of local interest, is believed to date from the fifteenth century but did not merit a mention from Upminster's first historian, T.L. Wilson in 1856 or 1881. Nor indeed did the Upminster Local History Group mention it in their historical booklets issued between 1957 and 1962.

Work was already well under way on the development of the Garden Suburb when this photograph looking south on Hall Lane was taken around 1911. Griggs wanted his suburb to 'preserve its healthy and rural condition and ... attract a desirable class of people'.

The saplings lining the avenue approaching Upminster Court show the mansion was still new in this photograph dating from 1911. It was built to the west of Hall Lane from 1905 onwards as a house for Arthur E. Williams, a director of Samuel Williams & Co. to the designs of Charles Reilly of High House. It is now used as a training venue and Capel Manor agricultural college.

Champion Road was part of the initial development of Upminster, the Branfill Park estate built by Dowsing & Davis of Romford from 1904 onwards. *Champion* was the name of Capt. Andrew Branfill's ship, and also the name he gave to his eldest son, born in 1683.

One of the first of the large detached houses built on Hall Lane by Griggs & Co. In November 1906 Griggs paid £20,000 for 150 acres on which to develop his Garden Suburb and the first brick was laid two weeks later. The dearest houses, such as this one, were sold freehold or on long leases for over £1,000.

The First World War brought development almost to a halt but this picture shows that by 1917, although well-wooded, Hall Lane had lost much of its rural charm.

Courtenay Gardens, shown here in 1911, was one of the first streets of the Garden Suburb developed east of Hall Lane a few years earlier. As with other roads, such as Waldegrave and Deyncourt Gardens, it took its name from a family who had Upminster connections in the Middle Ages.

Engayne Gardens looking south towards Waldegrave Gardens. These roads, together with Ashburnham Gardens, were built by Griggs on land stretching 920ft west of Hall Lane.

St Lawrence Road was recently finished at the time this photograph was taken in 1907 and these 'cottages' were being offered for sale at £245. The houses developed by Griggs south of the railway were more modest than those to the north and were aimed at a different market – artisans and traders rather than more middle-class professionals.

Unlike most roads in the Garden Suburb, Howard Road, photographed in 1911, was not named after local connections but took its name from Ebenezer Howard, who had pioneered the garden city movement, of which the Upminster Garden Suburb was an offshoot.

Griggs was an active developer and acquired much of the New Place estate, south of Cranham Road, in 1909 for £10,000. Building started in Argyle Gardens in 1921, and by 1927, the date of this photograph, building here was almost complete.

Work also began in 1921 on an extension of the Garden Suburb which took over ten years to complete. Ingrebourne and Deyncourt Gardens were extended eastwards and Claremont and Grosvenor Gardens had been added by the time this 1930s photograph of the latter road was taken.

The newly painted Wesleyan church in Hall Lane advertises its opening services on 9 July 1910. The church was established by members of the Seven Kings Methodist Church. They bought the site with 100ft frontage from Griggs and relocated a redundant iron church from Seven Kings to Upminster; unflatteringly it became known as the 'Tin Tabernacle'.

The Methodist congregation in Upminster started a building fund in 1920 to develop a church more in keeping with its surroundings. Work started in 1922 and in 1923 the current church replaced its iron predecessor, which was retained as the church hall at the rear.

three

Schooldays

Above: A class at the Girls' and Infants' School in Station Road, around 1910. In 1885 Upminster's two schools – the National School run by the Church of England and the British School run by the Nonconformists – were merged under a school board. The National School thereafter housed the boys' department, while the British School which stood opposite became home to girls and infants.

Left: The neglected British School buildings pictured a few years before their demolition in early 1938. The site was declared surplus by Essex County Council in 1936 and was sold at public auction for £6,400 the following year.

The old National School buildings in Station Lane in 1962, a few years before their demolition. The NatWest Bank now stands on the site. The school was built in 1851 and enlarged in 1897 with accommodation for 126 pupils.

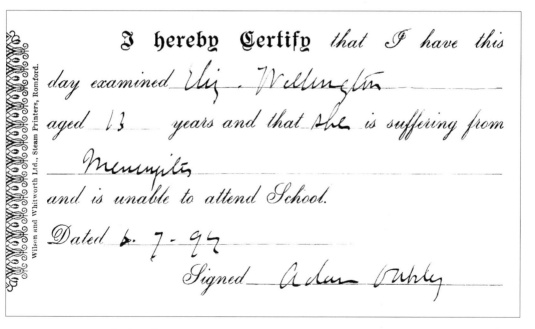

Wilson and Whitworth Ltd., Steam Printers, Romford.

I hereby Certify that I have this day examined *Miss Wellington* aged *13* years and that *she* is suffering from *Meningitis* and is unable to attend School.

Dated *6. 7 - 97*

Signed *A dan Oakley*

In Victorian and Edwardian times contagious diseases such as measles and diphtheria were common, and ill health was rife. This medical officer's certificate from 1897 from the Girls' and Infants' School shows that meningitis also made an appearance.

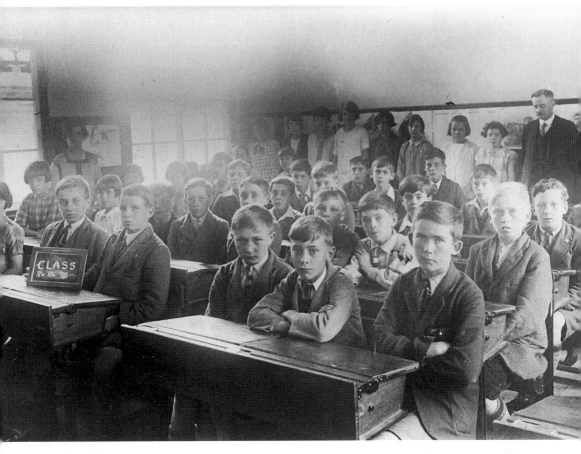

Above: A class photograph at Upminster Council School, 1928, with Mr F.J. Cox, headmaster, standing on the right at the back and Miss Lacey, class teacher, on the left. The boys in the front row are: ? Claxson, Charles Slocombe, Len Anglin, Basil Williams, ? Ward. The middle row from directly behind Len Anglin includes Les Carter, Vic Bradnam and ? Lazell, while at the far right are Bert Lee and ? Matthams.

Opposite above: Upminster Council School not long after its opening in April 1928. From the outset the school became known as the Bell School, as it was next to Upminster's prominent inn of that name. Essex County Council had bought the school site in order to build a 500-pupil school but it took years of pressure from Upminster Parish Council before work started in 1927.

Opposite below: Continued house building in Upminster meant that almost at once the new school was not big enough for the parish's rapidly growing population. Seven new classrooms and a hall were completed in March 1932 and even then portable buildings were kept in use. The 1928 buildings now form the Infants' School, with the newer extension constituting the Junior School.

Above: The cast of *Alice in Wonderland*, performed by pupils at Upminster High School, Hall Lane, on 12 December 1930. From left to right, back row: Dorothy Walmsley (Hatter) and Adeline Barber (White Rabbit). Standing: Mary Killingback (Mock Turtle), Pat Cook (Dodo), Betty Broad (Dormouse), Merle Allen (King of Hearts), Joyce Hansen (Alice), Doreen McPherson (Queen of Hearts), Percy Harwood (Executioner), Betty Compton (Cook) and Rita Hall (Cheshire Cat). Middle row: -?-, Ruth ?, -?-, Bryan Quinlan (Caterpillar), Iris Rumbold (Knave of Hearts), Margaret Killingback (Gardener), Joan Richards (Duchess). Front row: George Aggiss (Fish Footman), Phyllis George (Rabbit), -?-, Valerie Pilbeam, -?-, Elizabeth Hayward, -?-, -?-, -?-, -?-.

Opposite above: Miss Emma Browne, standing far right, with teachers and pupils at Upminster High School in the 1920s. Miss Browne opened the school for boarders and day pupils in a newly built detached house on the corner of Waldegrave Gardens and Hall Lane in October 1907. The Misses Parry took over in around 1929 when Miss Browne retired.

Opposite below: The former grand residence of Hill Place, rebuilt in 1872-73, was bought by the nuns of the Order of the Institute of the Sacred Heart of Mary in 1927 and was initially a private school for girls aged up to eight. It ceased to be a boarding school after the Second World War and since 1949 has been a voluntary aided Roman Catholic girls' school.

The actual location of Emerson Park School has not been confirmed but it is possible it was in Parkstone Avenue, Emerson Park. The period before the First World War was a golden age for small private schools and colleges, with no fewer than four listed in Hornchurch.

A class of boys, again at Emerson Park School. In the 1920s one such private school in Emerson Park was run by Mr Forde, an ex-Cambridge don, who, a former pupil recalled, was fond of Whitbread Pale Ale!

A display of decorated hoops at Miss Hatting's School, Emerson Park, July 1911. Lewis Hatting was listed as occupier of 'The Nest', Parkstone Avenue, from 1912 to 1928.

An infants' class from the Cottage Homes School, Hornchurch, July 1919. After 1924 the children from the Cottage Homes attended the school in North Street, after a government inspector reported unfavourably on the progress they made in their separate school.

Cranham Church School, 1922-23. From left to right, front row: Elsie Longsdale, George Cook, George Misson, Winnie Cook, ? Jones, Gwen Jones, Cissy Walker, ? Carter, Elsie Harrod, Rosemary Banks, Harry Dack. Middle row: Albert Oliff, Nobby Knock, John Walker, Charles Spillman, Annie Oliff, Enid Jones, Rosie Glessing, Phyllis Anderson, Joseph Edwards. Back row: Queenie Walker, Rosie Greenhill, Midge Bright, Kathleen Collins, Maggie Hasler, Ada Oliff, Edward Harrod, Mr Thorogood (headmaster).

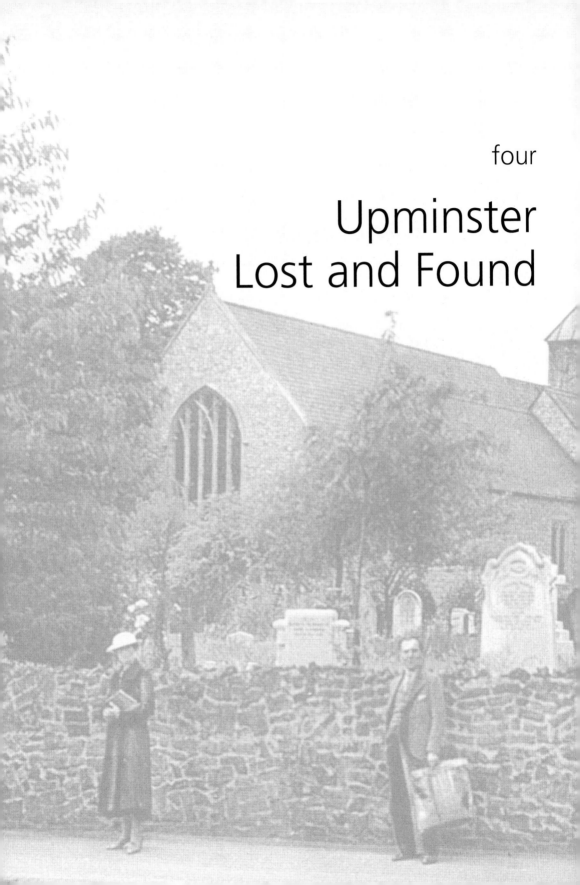

four

Upminster
Lost and Found

The junction of Hall Lane and Bird Lane, 1908. There was a sizeable community living in this area; many people were employed at the brickfields nearby to the east of Hall Lane, some of whom lived in the Pantile Cottages in Bird Lane, built in 1885 by the brickfields' leaseholder James Brown.

The notice board on Upminster or Tyler's Common, seen here around 1906, sets out the by-laws under which the parishioners could use the common of the Manor of Upminster Hall. The signpost at the Four Wantz corner points east to Warley, west up Shepherds Hill to Harold Wood and on to Romford, south back down Hall Lane to Upminster, and north up Nags Head Lane towards Brentwood.

Farm buildings at Hall Lane, Upminster Common, in 1908. The pond is likely to have been formed by earlier clay workings from the brickfield. In 1906 four farmers were named at Upminster Common: Horace Newte at Moat Farm, Henry Padfield at Page's and Great House Farms, Hugh Purvis at Vale Farm, and Daniel Shuttleworth at Ivy Lodge.

The Forge, Upminster Common, in about 1928. Arthur Prentice, a smith, had recently succeeded Edward Miller, who had occupied the forge since at least 1899; Miller was still in business just before the war. The hamlet was over two miles north of the village centre so the local smithy saved valuable time for local farmers.

Above: Described as the 'Old Cottages' on this photograph from the 1930s, these dwellings still survive on the east side of Hall Lane, north of the Arterial Road, now the A127. The opening of this road in 1925 cut off the north of the parish and made the hamlet at Upminster Common even more remote from the village, until the fly-over opened in 1966.

Above: Looking south down Corbets Tey Road from the Bell Corner, 1910. Upminster's local bobby, PC James Beasley, surveys the scene, while two young lads look on outside the church. PC Beasley was perhaps Upminster's best-known constable; he came to the parish in 1901, was promoted to sergeant in 1912 and left the parish when he was transferred to Harwich five years later.

Opposite below: Great Tomkyns Farm was once known as Great Readings. Pevsner described it as 'a good fifteenth-century yeoman's house with exposed timber framing'. Timber-framed houses date from the time before brick was used for house building; they are most common where oak was readily available and in the late eighteenth century much remaining timber from this estate was cut down for shipbuilding.

St Laurence's Church in the early 1920s. The church had undergone a major restoration sixty years before, in 1861-62, to the plans of Mr W.G. Bartleet of Brentwood. The Rector, John Rose Holden, contributed £1,000 towards the total building costs of £1,278. During the restoration, many items of historic worth were unfortunately disposed of, including the pulpit dating from 1740 and many ancient brasses.

The church in the late 1930s, after further major works in 1928-29, when the church was expanded for Upminster's growing population. The chancel was removed and a choir and sanctuary built at the east end, along with the choir aisle and St George's Chapel on the south side, and the Lady Chapel on the east end of the north aisle.

The church interior in the early 1920s. The Abbot of Waltham originally provided the octagonal font dating from the late fifteenth century for the chapel at Upminster Hall; Mr Champion Branfill presented it to the church when the chapel was dismantled in 1777. Some good examples of monumental brasses have survived, the oldest dating from 1455.

A snowy day at Upminster's Rectory Fields before 1920. The eighteen acres of glebeland, along Corbets Tey Road south of the parish church, were already used for sports by the parish when it was bought from the church for use as a recreation ground and public park in 1929.

CORBETS TEY ROAD, UPMINSTER

L 2132

Above: By 1950 the east side of Corbets Tey Road between High House and Hunts Farm had been redeveloped. Byron Parade (in the background) had replaced High House in 1935, while two rows of cottages, the older ones known as Post Office Cottages, were demolished in 1938. Just after the war this new parade including the Woolworth's store was built.

Opposite above: High House, which stood in Corbets Tey Road opposite the church, was built in around 1580. Its most famous occupant was the Revd William Derham who lived there from 1700 because of the poor state of repair of the Rectory. The last owner was Charles Reilly, who designed Upminster Court and died in 1928. High House was demolished in 1935 and was replaced by Byron Parade.

Opposite below: The square-fronted ten-bedroomed Hunts Farm on Corbets Tey Road in around 1920. The last occupier was Walter Joslin, brother of Henry Joslin, after whose death in 1927 Hunts and its eighty-one acres of farmland was offered for sale as part of the Gaynes estate.

Gaynes Cross, now 201 Corbets Tey Road, seen here in around 1906. This was the eastern lodge to the manor of Gaynes; the entrance to the estate can be seen on the right just off the junction with Little Gaynes Lane. In 1842 it was the site of the manor pound where stray animals were taken to await collection by their owners.

The manor house of Gaynes, a few years before the death in 1927 of the final owner Henry Joslin. This house had been rebuilt in 1846 by Revd George Clayton, and was smaller than its predecessor, built by Sir James Esdaile in 1771.

Gaynes Villa in around 1911. Also known as the Dower House, it was built in 1821 on the Gaynes estate by the lord of the manor, Revd John Clayton. After his death in 1843 it was occupied by Thomas Johnson, who had married the Revd Clayton's only daughter.

The Grade II listed bridge in Gaynes Parkway is now one of the few remaining relics of Sir James Esdaile's Gaynes Park estate. As part of his estate improvements Esdaile widened the stream which passed through the estate to make it into a boating lake; he also spent large sums on landscaping the grounds.

Above: Fox Hall in around 1920. With its high-pitched roof and prominent chimney stacks it is perhaps not surprising that Upminster's first historian Wilson described it as 'the first modern mansion of any pretensions erected in our parish'. It stood at the south end of Corbets Tey Road, opposite the current Parklands Avenue, and was demolished in the mid-1930s.

Left: High House, Corbets Tey, seen here in 1911, is one of Upminster's rare survivals from its age of elegance. Probably dating from the late seventeenth century – with parts from much earlier – it once commanded an impressive view, as there was an uninterrupted perspective across Gaynes Manor before the Park was laid out in the 1780s.

The 'Old Cottages', Corbets Tey, were formerly an inn named the George, until it closed in October 1901. In 1789 the inn was called the Royal George, and in 1835 the George and Dragon. The large hamlet of Corbets Tey once had five inns.

Looking west down Harwood Hall Lane, with Bearblock's Cottages on the left. The cinema billboard for the Towers in Hornchurch confirms it is 1935 or later, although top billing goes to Norma Shearer and Robert Montgomery in *Private Lives*, the film version of Noel Coward's play, which was released in 1931.

Harwood Hall was built in 1782 by Sir James Esdaile for his son-in-law George Stubbs (1738–1808), who is not to be confused with the famous painter of the same name who lived from 1724 to 1806, and who specialised in paintings of horses. The hall was enlarged in 1840 and the battlements were probably added later.

The cemetery at Corbets Tey opened in 1902. It was needed not only because the churchyard was becoming full but also because Upminster's large Nonconformist community sought a separate burial ground. The South Essex crematorium opened immediately to the west in 1957.

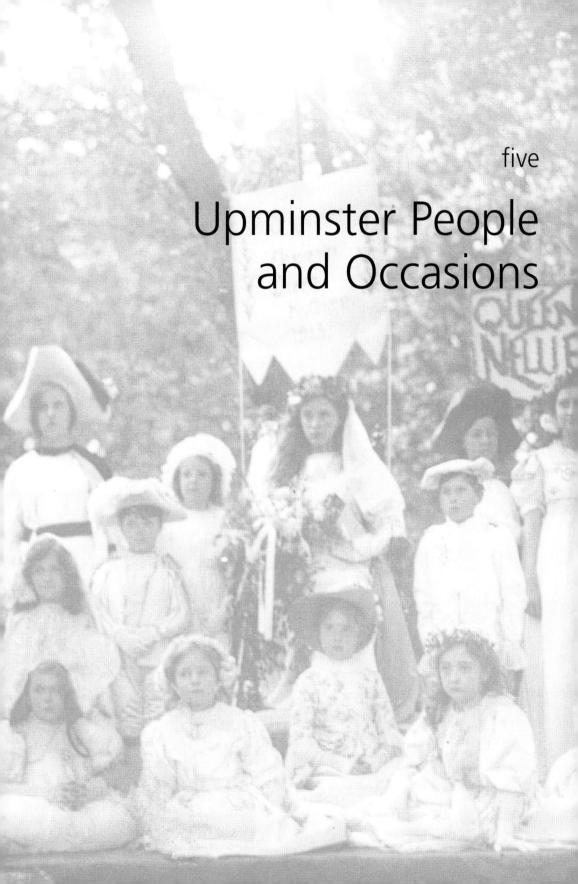

five

Upminster People and Occasions

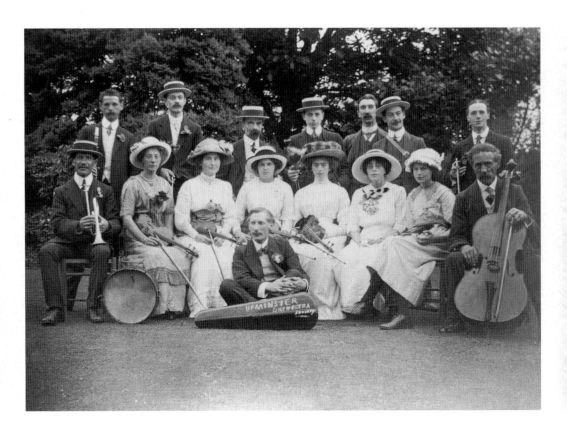

Above: The Revd Hyla Henry Holden, with his wife and children Hyla Rose, who succeeded his father as Rector in 1944, Kathleen and Paul. The Holden family's association with Upminster lasted almost 200 years from the appointment to the parish of Revd John Rose Holden in 1780 to the death of Hyla Rose Holden in 1971.

Opposite above: Upminster Orchestra Society in the Edwardian era. Many clubs and societies were formed after Upminster's population influx caused by the building of the Garden Suburb from 1906. This may well be one such amateur group who provided entertainment at concerts in the village and neighbouring areas.

Opposite below: The Glebe tennis club at the rear of the Rectory and St Laurence's Church. The Revd Hyla Holden was a keen sportsman and instituted many clubs and sporting activities for local young people at the parish church after he took over as Rector in 1904.

Celebrating the church bazaar, c.1925, although from their expressions many of the group don't seem to be enjoying the occasion! The church and its activities were at the heart of village life throughout the inter-war years.

The Cub Scout pack from St Laurence's Church in the mid-1920s. The pack was formed in 1917 and in the 1920s the curate Revd Lewis was Cubmaster. Fred Halestrap was a member of the original Scout pack, staying on for over thirty-five years to become Scoutmaster and Rover leader.

Upminster May Festival Queens, c.1927. The queens pictured in the front row are (left to right): Olive Gillings (1915), Phyllis Dean (1917), Madge Gillings (1920), Marjorie Turner (1918) and Mary Mason (1921). Also pictured are Betty Knight (1925), Betty King (1923), Hilda Halestrap (1922), and Edith Taylor (1924), and attendants.

The festival was instituted by the Revd Holden in 1913 and continued right up to the Second World War. The May Queen, who was aged fifteen or sixteen, was typically chosen from members of the church Sunday School. The first May Queen was Kathleen, the Revd Holden's daughter, who is shown here with her court.

This is believed to be the May Queen for 1917, Phyllis Dean. Each year the queens from earlier years took part in the celebrations, which included a church service and procession up and down Station Road.

As befitted a May celebration, the festivities included dancing round the maypole. Despite popular belief there is no evidence that maypoles were connected to pagan worship – although seventeenth-century Puritan reformers disapproved of the dancing and merry-making that ensued.

Queen of Roses Tableau. It seems likely that this entertainment was linked to the annual May Festival, or possibly another local celebration. The hairstyles suggest a date around the First World War.

Mr Rogers and four exotically dressed characters from the Orient. Again the occasion may well be Upminster's May Festival. Mr Rogers, who lived at 55 Howard Road around 1920, is believed to be the photographer of the following series of pictures of the 1919 Peace celebrations.

Upminster's Peace celebrations, 1919. Towns and villages all over the land celebrated the end of the Great War. Upminster's population obviously entered fully into the swing of things with none too serious an approach – the Jack Tar on the right wears a costume covered in Navy Cut and Weights cigarette packets.

These girls taking part in the 1919 Peace celebrations display the traditional costumes of Britain's war allies, the French, Dutch, Belgians and Spanish.

The Peace parade passing down Howard Road, as 'Tommies' flank the Kaiser who is in a spiked helmet. Among those following is someone in a splendid cavalier's costume.

The gentleman on the left may well be Henry Joslin of Gaynes Park, Deputy Lieutenant of Essex. The troop of nurses is no doubt from Upminster's auxiliary hospital, which fulfilled a vital role in the newly built St Laurence's Hall. Miss Sophia Reilly was the Assistant Commandant who did much to make the hospital a success.

Above: Some members of the Locust Club, Easter 1925. It is unclear what the club actually did but it involved several prominent parishioners who were also members of the church choir. The adults standing are, from left to right: Revd Hyla Henry Holden, –?–, Paul Holden, Ted Pearmain, Ernest Hills, Mrs Sykes, Ernest 'Tiny' Gates, ? Ebblewhite or Hepplewhite, Mrs Norledge, Frank Norledge MBE, Hyla Rose Holden, George Taylor. Children seated: ? Sykes, ? Holden, ? Sykes, ? Holden.

Opposite above: A superbly decorated horse-drawn haulage vehicle operated by William 'Billy' Aggiss at the Chestnuts, opposite Bell Corner. Aggis had started as a jobmaster behind the Bell in around 1890 hiring out horses and cabs – he always preferred horses and kept them for hire even after the First World War ended. It was his son Henry James Aggiss who first invested in a truck after 1918. The business expanded into other areas, including motor engineering and petrol sales.

Opposite below: Opening of the new Roomes store, Station Road, 4 May 1937. James Roome developed his original draper's store in Green Street, Upton Park, in 1888. He and his family moved to the newly-built 16 Engayne Gardens, Upminster in 1908 but he died unexpectedly five years later. The firm expanded under his son Millice ('Mill') Roome and in 1927 their first Upminster store opened. This was enlarged in 1930 and fully rebuilt as a department store in 1936-37.

Upminster fire brigade, *c.*1927. A volunteer brigade was formed in 1909 and seven fire hydrants were installed in the parish. The volunteers were paid 3s an hour when working on a fire and 1s 6d when working subsequently, although payment for drills amounted to 5s between the whole brigade, or just a few pence for each man. The brigade's efficiency improved when a retired fire officer, Mr John Bridger, was appointed as captain in 1925.

Upminster fire engine, *c.*1927. Initially the Upminster brigade had only a hand-truck at their disposal and the more effective Hornchurch brigade were called to any major incidents. This caused bad feeling and several disputes, and the parish council were unhappy about the costs incurred. Eventually in 1927 the parish council bought the brigade its first motorised fire engine.

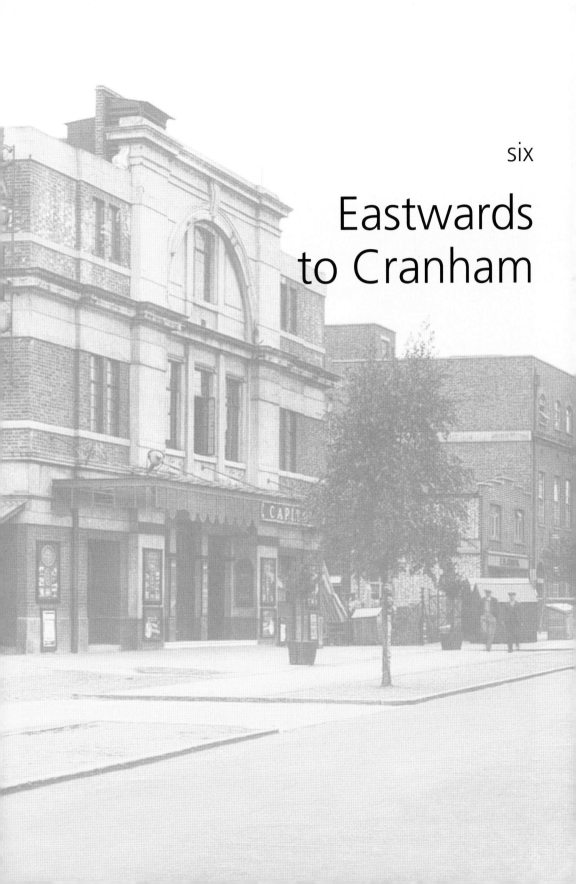

six

Eastwards
to Cranham

A still rural Cranham Lane, just east of the Bell junction, in 1910. Already W.P. Griggs' plans to redevelop this area were under way and by the early 1920s this country lane had succumbed to bricks and mortar. It was renamed St Mary's Lane, taking its title from the chapel in St Laurence's Church.

St Mary's Lane, looking towards Bell corner in the early 1930s, only a few years after this parade opened opposite Sunnyside Gardens. Mr Leslie Wylie started his veterinary surgeon's business from a flat above A.W. Sibley's butchers from 1936.

St Mary's Lane in the late 1930s. Cramphorn's corn and flour merchant occupies the low building, next to David Ramsey's newsagents (203 St Mary's Lane) which was established in Oak Place, which was originally a private house dating from 1740. Next along was Samuel Nurse's pastry cook's, then Eastman's cleaner's, and the United Dairies.

St Mary's Lane from the junction with Sunnyside Gardens around 1950. The petrol pumps on the left show that the corner plot was in use as the garage which still remains.

Thomas Anglin's fish merchant's business originated in St Mary's Lane, before relocating to 46 Station Road in later years. Mr Anglin – an appropriate name for a fish merchant – is on the left, and the even more appropriately named Jim Whiting, is pictured with him.

The Regent tobacconist, at 174 St Mary's Lane, in the 1950s. This shop on the south side of the road, by the telephone exchange, is now an Indian restaurant. The telephone exchange and other premises nearby opened in 1929.

The Capitol Cinema, which opened in St Mary's Lane in 1929, is showing Bert Wheeler and Robert Woolsey in *The Rainmakers* (1935). On the far right the sign shows Drury and Archer's builders, who were located at 217 St Mary's Lane. The Capitol, later named the Gaumont, was demolished in 1974 to make way for a supermarket, now Somerfield.

Cranham Road, outside New Place, looking towards Cranham, in 1908. On the north side of the road are some of the new homes built by W.P. Griggs as part of the more modest southern sector of the Garden Suburb.

Looking through the sweeping entrance to New Place, 1910. New Place was the last and grandest of Sir James Esdaile's buildings in Upminster, erected in 1775. By 1910 the estate had been sold to W.P. Griggs for development and the house itself was demolished in 1924 after the death of the last tenant John Wilson, former Chief Engineer of the Great Eastern Railway.

Clockhouse, the former stable block of New Place, was bought for use as offices for Upminster's Parish Council. The sale went ahead in January 1925 after almost two years of wrangling. The building takes its name from the clock, which is reputed to come from the Admiralty Superintendent's house at Woolwich.

The Clockhouse Gardens, seen here in the early 1950s, remain a quiet spot that bear memories of their former glory as the private gardens of Esdaile's New Place. The branches of one of Esdaile's landmark cedar trees used to hang down over the moat while at least two other cedars graced the grounds.

The Mason's Arms, Cranham Road, in 1908. Benjamin White was listed as the beer retailer in the first decades of the twentieth century. The current premises were built in 1928. The pub marks the easternmost part of Upminster parish along the redeveloped St Mary's Lane.

Central Cranham, showing Moor Lane just before the war. The houses in the background were completed in 1931, while the gas lamp-post may have survived a few years after the arrival of the electricity main in 1933. Moor Lane was previously named Back Lane; the current name only came into use in the late nineteenth century with the old form often still used as late as 1920.

The south elevation of Cranham Hall in the 1930s. This is the fourth hall, built around 1790-91, but with a known major remodelling in 1812. It appears to retain the front door and porch from the third hall, a larger, red-bricked building dating from around two centuries earlier.

seven

Upminster to Hornchurch

LODGE
COURT

Left: Harold Moore (left) was apprenticed aged fifteen to William H. Rowe at the grocer's shop at Ivy House, Upminster Hill, around 1893. He married Alice Rowe, daughter of William Frederick Rowe, in 1907, and worked at the store through several changes of ownership until his retirement in 1957, aged seventy-nine.

'Phone: UPMINSTER 94

H. A. MOORE

HILL STORES UPMINSTER

FOR

Groceries & Provisions

of Dependable Quality

WINES, SPIRITS and BOTTLED BEERS

Right: Advertisement for Harold Moore's store in the 1930s. As well as groceries and a wide range of provisions, the store also sold wines, spirits and beers. A price list from the early 1930s shows Scotch whiskies for 12s 6d (62½p) a bottle, Martell's brandy at 17s 6d (87½p) and a quart of Whitbread's India Pale Ale retailing for 1s 1d (less than 6p).

A bus crests the top of Upminster Hill on its way from Hornchurch in the early 1930s. In earlier days the steep climb up out of the Ingrebourne Valley had often proved a difficult haul for well-laden horse-drawn vehicles.

Newly built houses on Hornchurch Road, later renamed St Mary's Lane, in around 1907. These houses stood just west of the original post office, opposite the church. The site is now occupied by St Joseph's RC Primary School.

Left: Upminster windmill was still in active use when pictured here in 1917. The Abraham brothers – Clement, Alfred and Thomas – ran the mill and related coal merchant's business. Clement was the business manager, Alfred the miller and Thomas ran the coal merchant's on Upminster station approach.

Below: By the early 1950s the mill was in a dilapidated state. After Clement Abraham's death in 1935 the mill was offered for sale and was eventually bought by Essex County Council but not before a decade of neglect. The mill's condition continued to worsen and major maintenance was only carried out in 1962–63.

Thomas Wilson (1833-1919), on the right, outside the Bridge House around 1908. Wilson was just twenty-three when he wrote his first Upminster history in 1856, fully revising it in 1881. He was by trade a builder, although he turned his hand to most things: in addition to his parish history he compiled six invaluable volumes of historical cuttings about Upminster. Like many smaller pubs, the Bridge House originated as a beer house.

Above and below: The GEM confectioners, stationers and tobacconists at 31 Upminster Road, Hornchurch, was bought by Ernest Foord after he left the London Electric Wire Company at Leyton in 1952. It was a profitable business but he sold it in 1956 for health reasons. The shop forms part of the parade near the junction with Wingletye Lane.

Hacton Lane runs south from the crossroads with Wingletye Lane continuing towards the hamlet of Hacton. Hacton Bridge, across the Ingrebourne, divides the parishes of Hornchurch and Upminster and this was a very old site for a bridge. The upkeep was shared between the Manor of Gaynes and the County of Essex.

Old houses at Hay Green, Wingletye Lane, Hornchurch. Wingletye Lane was known as Hay Street as early as 1438; the name comes from the Anglo Saxon word hay, meaning enclosure. The road (or chase) which runs off to the right leads to Lilliputs Farm, which dates from the sixteenth century.

Dury Falls House, another building surviving from the sixteenth century, stands at the junction with Wingletye Lane. In the past the house was often known as Doggett's, and the junction as Doggett's Corner, after an eighteenth century occupier. Dury Falls is now again known by its original name. Thomas Gardner JP, who played a prominent part in parish affairs, owned it during the first decades of the twentieth century.

Hornchurch Hall in the early twentieth century. The Hall, which stood opposite the church, was described in 1923 as a sixteenth-century house with a seventeenth-century chimney, and a large modern addition on the south front. The Hornchurch Hall estate was sold for development from 1927 and the house itself was demolished in 1941 after sustaining wartime bomb damage.

Hornchurch Mill in around 1906. The mill stood south of the church and was in use by Thomas and George Howard until 1912, but was burnt down in 1921. It was one of three ancient corn mills in Hornchurch, the others being on the manors of Dovers and Mardyke.

The Mill Cottage in the Dell, adjacent to the Mill Fields, in 1917. It is a timber-framed building dating back at least to the seventeenth century. The Dell was a popular local beauty spot which also served as a venue for sporting events, including the famous prize fight between Mendoza the Jew and John Jackson in 1795.

The Revd Herbert Dale, his curate Revd Alfred Tibble and views of the church, around 1912. The living at St Andrew's, Hornchurch, was endowed by New College, Oxford, which received the income from Hornchurch Hall and Suttons Farms. The College appointed the vicar, who was a member of the College. The local clergyman was described as 'Vicar Temporal' and regarded as a chaplain to the parishioners.

A horse and trap stands outside St Andrew's Church, 1917. Nothing survives of the church which existed from 1163 when Henry II gave it to the newly established Hornchurch Priory. In its present form it originates from the early thirteenth century, but was modified two centuries later, and again in 1802.

Wykeham Cottage, seen here in the 1930s, commemorates the strong link with New College, and its founder William of Wykeham, Bishop of Winchester. Wykeham is believed to have built the tower of St Andrew's Church in the last years of the fourteenth century.

Lodge Court stands on the site of Hornchurch Lodge (demolished 1937) which was said by Perfect to be a 'beautiful ivy-covered old house in the middle of Church Hill … in all probability built some time in the sixteenth century.' Thomas Mashiter occupied it for much of the nineteenth century, after which Dr Thomas Lambe lived there.

Looking towards the King's Head and Hornchurch village in the 1930s. Until the 1950s Hornchurch retained its ancient village charm but many remaining old buildings were swept away. Fortunately this did not include the building in the centre of the picture, then occupied by the Cottage Tea Rooms, which has survived and is now a restaurant.

The offices of Hornchurch Brewery are on the left. Founded by Thomas Woodfine around 1789, the business grew and at its peak employed over sixty staff. The brewery and all its tied houses was bought by Mann, Crossman & Paulin in 1925, about five years after this picture was taken.

eight

Hornchurch Village

The old cottages at the west end of the High Street, 1917. These lath-and-plaster cottages along with adjacent buildings were demolished in 1938. Hornchurch's historian Charles Perfect described the High Street that he first knew around 1902 as a 'picturesque street, with its cobbled sidewalks'.

The High Street, looking east, around 1925. Arthur Wakeham's grocer's is the shop on the right, while next door is Charles Evans' Brooklands Farm Dairy, which superseded the earlier Moss Brothers Dairy. It was often possible to buy milk fresh from the cow as Evans' herd grazed in a field behind the shop.

Above: The old archway and cottages in the village centre in about 1908. Perfect described them as 'undoubtedly of sixteenth-century origin' but they may have been of even greater antiquity.

Right: The archway stands derelict, with its roof timbers exposed prior to its demolition in 1937. The redevelopment of Hornchurch gathered pace in the decade before the Second World War, just as it did in Upminster. After escaping Hitler's bombs the destruction continued for the decades after the war until the 'improvements' were complete.

In the background is the Bull Inn, while beyond can be seen Page Calnan's builders' merchants, which occupied the former site of Wedlake's Union Iron Foundry. The photographer has attracted a small crowd of boys, some sitting outside this terrace of cottages and shops, including far right Frank Hill's baker's and confectioner's.

A similar view to the previous photograph, but taken over thirty years later, around 1950. In contrast to the traffic-free streets of the earlier view, this scene has more of a bustling air and the village feel is giving way to an emerging shopping centre.

Looking west in the early 1930s. On the right is the Britannia (sic) Tea Rooms, while in the background the Hovis sign marks Robert Beard's baker's shop, and the garage sign is probably for Easter's motor engineers who took over from Frost Brothers. On the south side of the road the Hornchurch and District Sick Animal Dispensary can be seen.

Hornchurch High Street in the 1960s. The prominent Burton's store on the corner of North Street was built in 1939, while the Fine Fare supermarket shows how shopping habits are changing. The shop with the blind was United Dairies, while next door to that for many years was Luff's tobacconist's. Frank Luff is best known for his outstanding series of photographs recording Hornchurch's past.

The former Britannia Inn, which closed in 1907. This photograph dates from a few years before the inn's demolition in March 1938 to make way for Burton's. The inn was reputedly of very ancient origins and a rest place for monks. The last occupiers claimed to have seen an apparition of a ghostly monk dressed in a brown habit.

Looking towards the village centre from the southern end of North Street in the early 1930s. The varied nature of the buildings and architectural styles obviously added to its charm but failed to stop the march of progress.

Cottages on North Street, *c.*1906. North Street runs from Hornchurch village northwards towards Emerson Park, joining Billet Lane and forming Butts Green Road. By around 1900 a series of villas, houses and cottages had been built.

North Street in the early 1930s. Thomas Wedlake and his family owned much land around here, opposite the Queen's Theatre and north of the current fire station. Their ironworks and engineering business moved there in 1894, continuing until around 1937.

Left: Billet Lane, close to Hornchurch village, in 1910 or earlier. Until 1877 an annual fair was held in the village on Whit Monday. Booths were set up in the High Street and a merry-go-round was sited at the High Street end of Billet Lane, near the workhouse pond, which would have been just out of this picture on the left.

Below: A milk delivery in the snow, Fairkytes, Billet Lane, *c.*1916. This eighteenth-century house was the home of Thomas Wedlake, whose iron foundry was opposite. Joseph Fry, son of the prison reformer Elizabeth Fry, lived here in the late Victorian period. It was later bought by Hornchurch UDC who opened a library there in 1953.

The Foundry Cottage in the early 1930s. This was the office for Wedlake's iron foundry which stood opposite Fairkytes, on land which is now part of the Queen's Theatre. It reminds us of the days when Hornchurch was very much an industrial village with a well-regarded ironworks supplying the agricultural trade around a wide area, and a popular brewery.

Langtons, Billet Lane, in the late 1930s. This twenty-two-room red brick mansion dates from the mid-eighteenth century and replaced a much older house. Mr Varco Williams JP bought the house from Col. Holmes in 1899 and remodelled it. Mr Williams and his daughter, Mrs Elizabeth Parkes, gifted the house and grounds to Hornchurch UDC for use as offices in 1929.

Above: A road-making gang and steamroller behind the White Hart, Station Lane, 1920s. The workmen have paused from their labours, and a group of local children look on. Although tarmac – small stones bound together with tar – had been developed for road making over a century before, in the early twentieth century most local roads still had a rolled gravel surface so the tarmac surface the men are laying was still somewhat of a novelty.

Opposite above: Looking east past the King's Head, *c.*1950. Although heavily restored after a fire in 1966, the pub retains the aura of its origins in the late seventeenth century; it also later served as a coaching inn. Not surprisingly beer and spirits were supplied by the Hornchurch Brewery opposite, whose workers frequented the premises.

Opposite below: Can anyone identify these two distinguished gentlemen standing outside the White Hart on a snowy day before 1920? This red-brick hostelry was built to replace a fourteenth- or fifteenth-century inn with gables and an overhanging front, which burned down in 1872. In turn this building was replaced in 1935 by the present premises.

Above: Hornchurch Carnival, August 1911. The carnival was a popular annual event and the procession featured many interesting contributions. This group are wearing original uniforms of parish officers from the early nineteenth century, with a constable, watch officer and volunteer fire brigade. The parish fire brigade was instituted in 1830 when the vestry bought a fire engine for £18 10s.

Opposite above: The top end of Station Lane, 1917. Rumsey's cycle and repair shop is out of picture on the left, while out of picture on the right were the still tranquil beer gardens of the White Hart. Raymond Rumsey opened his shop in 1919 and died aged eighty-four in 1952.

Opposite below: Shops and businesses behind the White Hart in Station Lane around 1950. Until the redevelopment of the junction to improve traffic flow the road leading directly into Station Lane from the west of the village was a narrow lane.

Mill Park tennis club, Station Lane. The Mill Park estate, developed just before the First World War on land formerly part of Hornchurch Lodge, took its name from the adjacent mill. A path from the Dell still leads through to Mill Park Avenue. These tennis courts survived in a dilapidated state until their redevelopment for housing a few years ago.

Wasps' nest, found in the gardens of the Bull Hotel in 1911. The caption indicates that there were ten tiers of comb. George Heath was the publican at that time. Despite the large size this nest would have been the product of a single summer's work by a swarm of wasps, as nests are discarded by the autumn, when most of the swarm dies.

The former Hornchurch cinema was converted shortly before this picture was taken to house the Queen's Theatre, named in favour of the recently crowned monarch in September 1953. The cinema was begun by three local businessmen in 1913 but foundered after Upminster's new Capitol Cinema opened in 1929. After various temporary uses, the old cinema was bought by Hornchurch UDC in 1948.

Devonshire Road, *c.*1906. Modern development started in central Hornchurch from around 1898 onwards with building by Joseph Turner on the west side of Station Lane, just south of the White Hart. The first roads to be built were The Avenue and Stanley Road with Devonshire Road built a few years later.

Suttons Gate stood on Station Lane, just north of the junction with Suttons Lane. Until the 1830s there was a gate across the roadway and the southward continuation of the lane was a private road to Suttons Farm. Robert Beard the butcher was the final owner, demolishing the house for development in 1936.

Suttons Lane, originally known as Blind Lane, ran west from Station Lane to join up with Abbs Cross Lane. It was developed for housing in the 1920s and in this photograph from that period the road remains narrow and unmade.

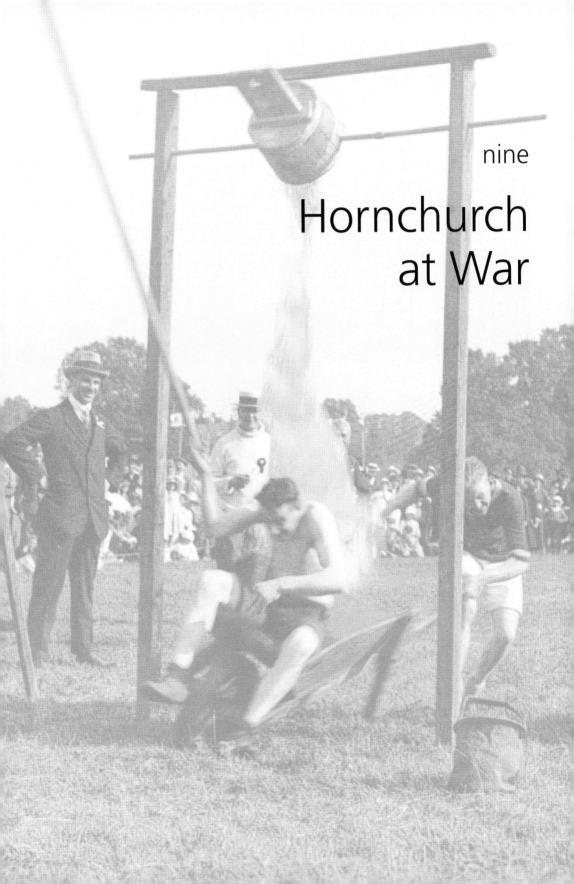

nine

Hornchurch
at War

Above: The Ravensbourne Brook, which is a tributary of the River Rom, ran through the grounds of the Grey Towers estate crossing under the Hornchurch Road at Raven's Bridge. The estate was formed from Mr John Wagener's Langton estate for his daughter Emilie, and her husband Henry Holmes, who married in 1863.

Left: The lake at Grey Towers was formed by damming the Ravensbourne Brook. Perfect described in 1917 the 'beautiful terrace gardens leading down to an ornamental lake', seen here around 1910. The house was the centre of social life in the village, hosting many celebrations.

Grey Towers mansion, a few years before the estate was sold for development in 1929. Henry Holmes built the castellated mansion in 1876 and moved there from the similarly styled Harwood Hall in Upminster. Col. Holmes – who commanded the Corps of the Essex Artillery Volunteers which he raised in 1882 – died in December 1913 and his wife died four months later.

The entrance gates of Grey Towers in late 1914 or early 1915. The gateposts matched the style of the house, as did the lodge. Like many estates all over Britain, Grey Towers was pressed into military use during the First World War. The sign records that the estate now hosts the headquarters of the Sportsman's Battalion of the Royal Fusiliers.

Above: The Sportsmen drilling as part of their training for war. They played a full part in village life and locals were invited to the regular social functions, many of them entertainments in aid of charitable causes. They departed from Hornchurch on 26 June 1915 to finish their training at Clipstone Camp.

Opposite above: The Sportsman's Battalion under the command of Col. Viscount Maitland arrived at Hornchurch with great ceremony on the afternoon of 4 November 1914. For weeks before their arrival hundreds of workmen were engaged to erect huts for the troops' accommodation and when completed it was regarded as a model camp.

Opposite below: The men of Hut 32 at Grey Towers, December 1914. This unique battalion was raised by Mrs Cunliffe-Owen and by royal dispensation men up to forty-five years old could enrol. The Sportsmen were all exponents of British sport, including famous men, and although most enrolled as 'Tommies' the battalion served as an Officers' Training Corps.

The band of the Sportsman's Battalion at the top of Station Lane, *c.*1914. When trenching work was done at a distance the band headed the march to and from the station. They also led the Sunday parade when the Sportsmen attended the service at St Andrew's Church. There was a succession of concerts and entertainments in aid of charitable causes while the battalion was based at Grey Towers.

Band of the New Zealand contingent, *c.*1917. Just as with the Sportsmen, the New Zealanders' band was often seen locally. One well-documented occasion was the celebrations for the first anniversary of Anzac Day on Easter Sunday, 23 April 1916, when the band, under Regimental Bandmaster Mahoney, headed a march to the church through the village.

Grey Towers was unoccupied for over four months after the Sportsmen's departure before the 26th Middlesex (the 'Navvies') Battalion were there briefly in late 1915. In January 1916 the New Zealand forces selected Grey Towers as their depot in England and the first batches of wounded men arrived. By summer 1916 Grey Towers was in full swing as a convalescent hospital.

Men of the New Zealand forces outside the imposing front entrance to Grey Towers, early 1918. The mansion itself served as the officers' quarters, just as it had during the stay of the Sportsman's Battalion in 1914-15.

A nurse and patients inside one of the hospital wards at Grey Towers, probably Christmas 1917 or 1918. The hospital had been set up to cope with 1,500 patients but was soon expanded to 2,000 as the original limit was found to be inadequate. Even then, more accommodation was needed to cope with all the New Zealanders needing to convalesce and the capacity was raised to 2,500.

The main avenue through the Convalescent Hospital, showing the YMCA building on the left and some huts on the right. When they were first opened in 1914 there were fifty separate buildings, laid out in streets. The timber barrack huts were well ventilated, standing well above the ground, and each contained thirty beds. The whole 'town' was lit by electricity.

Above: Ladies from the Hornchurch YMCA at Grey Towers camp, *c.*1918. The YMCA established a large hut, extended on several occasions, including a canteen, billiard room, a large hall seating over 800 people, a large reading and writing room, and a workshop which served as an arts and crafts department. The ladies not only cooked and served in the canteen but also taught basket-weaving.

Right: The New Zealand Soldiers' Club (known as 'Te Whare Puni' – the meeting house) at Beethoven House, Butts Green Road, 1917. This was opened in April 1914 as a place where soldiers could rest and eat home-made food and refreshments at a modest charge, which only covered the materials. Labour was all voluntarily provided by ladies, mainly local but some of New Zealand birth.

Above: The board says 'Ninth Canterbury Reinforcements, Hornchurch, 21.11.1917' but it is not obvious if this group of New Zealand Servicemen, pictured outside the ivy-covered front of Grey Towers, are arriving or departing.

Opposite above: Grey Towers Sports Day *c.*1915. The presence of an English army officer perhaps suggests that this celebration dates to the period when the Sportsman's Battalion was at Grey Towers.

Opposite below: This is thought to be a garden party given by Mrs M. Gardner at Dury Falls on Peace Day, 19 July 1919. The ladies are from the local branch of Queen Mary's Needlework Guild, which became known as the Hornchurch and Upminster War Hospital Supply Depot and Working Parties. They worked tirelessly from October 1915 onwards to raise funds to buy material which was made into surgical dressings, bandages etc.

Baby competition and garden party at Hornchurch Lodge, July 1919. This occasion at Dr Lambe's Hornchurch Lodge marked a ceremony at which prizes were distributed for a baby competition organised by the Maternity and Child Care Committee. Mrs Lambe was Secretary of the Hornchurch Committee, set up in 1918 by the Romford Rural District Council under an Act of Parliament.

Another scene from the garden party at Hornchurch Lodge in July 1919. The Hornchurch Committee was based at the Council Hall, Billet Lane and its role was to establish baby clinics and crèches, provide doctors and nurses for expectant mothers, and supply milk. The Medical Officer of Health attended fortnightly meetings to advise on children's illness and health and by 1919 attendance averaged twenty-eight mothers.

Right: Officers and boys from the Hornchurch Company of the Church Lads' Brigade outside St Andrew's Church, *c.*1910. The Brigade became a recognised unit of the Territorial Force in 1911 and at the outset of war practically all members of military age enlisted. Horace James Seccombe (second left) enlisted on November 1915 as a lieutenant with the 3rd Monmouth Regiment. He was severely wounded at Arras in April 1917 but remained in the army until May 1919.

Below: Church Lads' Brigade camp, possibly at Suttons Farm, *c.*1910. Major J.M. Ewing formed the Brigade in September 1903 to provide a leisure interest on weekdays and religious instruction on Sundays for village lads aged between thirteen and nineteen. They were successful from the outset, winning battalion trophies for efficiency in military exercises, shooting and sports.

William Leefe Robinson became a national hero overnight when he was the first airman to shoot down a German airship on 3 September 1916 after taking off from Suttons Farm. Within five days he was invested with the Victoria Cross by the King at Windsor Castle and was promoted to Captain. Lt Frederick Sowrey received the DSO for the same feat three weeks later.

The entrance to the RAF camp, Hornchurch, around 1960, just two years before the camp closed on 1 July 1962. Its proud history dates back to the establishment of a temporary landing ground for the Royal Flying Corps at Suttons Farm in spring 1915. From here Lt William Leefe Robinson earned his Victoria Cross for shooting down a German airship in 1916 and famous RAF pilots fought the Battle of Britain in 1940.

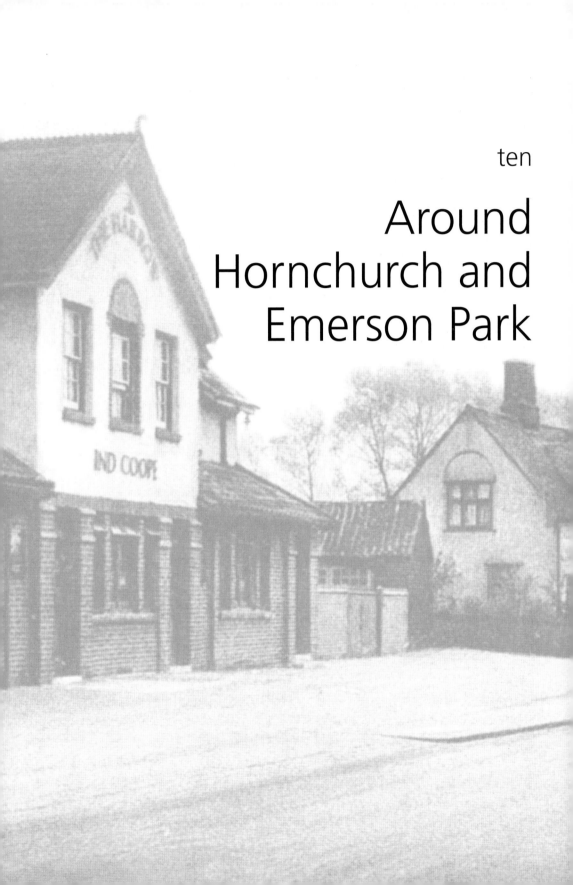

ten

Around Hornchurch and Emerson Park

Above: William and Eliza Carter and their three sons, Emerson, Herbert and Charles. William Carter named the estate he developed in Hornchurch after his eldest son Emerson (b.1880). He had many interests, among them cycling, and he organised road races near the family home in Parkstone, Dorset, as well as taking his sons on long cycle journeys, including cycling to London and back in a day. He was also a globe-trotter who founded a travel club, organising and leading trips to Switzerland and Italy. His close friendship with Ebenezer Howard, the originator of the Garden City concept, led to his developments at Emerson Park.

Opposite above: Parkstone Avenue, *c.*1906. This is one of the main roads through Carter's Emerson Park estate. It was named after William Carter's home town – the family lived in a house in Parkstone called the Hermitage, which commanded fine views across Poole Harbour. Plots averaging an acre each were sold from July 1895 and 109 houses were built or under way by 1901.

Opposite below: Ernest Road, *c.*1906. Its name is probably derived from the middle name of Charles Carter. There were constant struggles between the 'pioneer' occupiers of these new houses and Romford Rural District Council, the local authority. There were no links to mains drainage or sewers until after 1899, nor any refuse collection in these early years.

Bungalows at Curtis Road, *c.*1906. William Horner Cowley Curtis was William Carter's main agent locally at Emerson Park, living in one of the first houses built in Berther Road. Like Carter he hailed from Poole and it can be little coincidence that the two were closely connected. These bungalows were probably built speculatively for sale, rather than to order.

Great Nelmes estate, mid-1920s. Alfred Barber bought land from the Nelmes Park estate directly north of Emerson Park in 1904. He lived in Nelmes Manor House and developed plans for the rest, to be called the Great Nelmes estate. Woodlands Avenue, Elm Grove and Sylvan Avenue were the main roads, and this wooded estate preserved many mature trees.

A 252B bus in Butts Green Road in around 1935. Numbered DA45, this was one of three Dennis Dart-built buses with bodies by Metcalfe. It was built in 1933 for the Romford & District Company, which was taken over by London Transport in 1934. Route 252B ceased in December 1936.

Burnthouse Corner, in the 1930s. This house in traditional Essex clapperboard style survives at the junction between Butts Green Road and Slewins Lane.

Hilbery, Chaplin & Co., 93 South Street, Romford.

Semi-detached Freehold Houses

with extremely attractive elevations with half timbered front and mansard roof.

They occupy a quiet position on a country road known as

SLEWINS LANE, GIDEA PARK.

5 minutes walk from Gidea Park Station, with fast trains to London.

Room for the erection of a Garage if desired. Run in at rear.

Two minutes from 'buses to all parts and close to shops.

The accommodation is well arranged and comprises :—

GROUND FLOOR.

PANELLED SQUARE HALL, with casement windows.

DRAWING ROOM.—14 ft. 4 ins. by 13 ft. 3 ins. exclusive of 5-window bay, with expensive tiled fireplace.

DINING ROOM.—13 ft. 7 ins. by 10 ft. 9 ins. with modern tiled fireplace, with high pressure boiler at rear. Large cupboard. French doors to garden.

KITCHENETTE, tiled to a height of 5 feet and fitted with deep sink (h. & c.), draining board, enclosed dresser. Larder with tiled shelf. Power plug. Outside coal box.

FIRST FLOOR.

BEDROOM No. 1.—13 ft. 9 ins. by 11 ft. 3 ins. with lattice casement windows, tiled fireplace and hanging cupboard.

BEDROOM No. 2.—11 ft. 7 ins. by 12 ft. with tiled fireplace and airing cupboard.

BEDROOM No. 3.—9 ft. by 6 ft. 9 ins.

BATHROOM, tiled in colour to a height of 5 ft. 6 ins. and fitted with porcelain enamelled bath (h. & c.), soap tray let in wall, porcelain lavatory basin (h. & c.). Separate W.C.

Good Gardens in rear.

Electric fittings including f......witches supplied down to the holders.

10 per cent. Deposit.   ●   ## Price £725 Freehold.

NO ROAD CHARGES.

Company's Gas, Water and Electric Light. Main Drainage.

Left: Advertisement for houses in Slewins Lane, probably dating from the 1930s. These chalet-style three-bedroom semi-detached houses on the main route were of better quality than many in the area. The developers' description of the address as Gidea Park and the emphasis on the five-minute walk to the railway station suggests that these were marketed at London commuters.

Below: Slewins Lane in the early 1950s. The lane took its name from Slewings Farm (as it was spelt), which was sited north of the junction with Butts Green Road. Much of the development to the south of this old winding route on Great Gardens Farm was from 1928 onwards by the Standen Brothers, who were prolific builders in Hornchurch in the inter-war period.

The Squirrels Head, Ardleigh Green Road. Squirrels Heath, the area to the east of Gidea Park station (opened 1911) and west of Ardleigh Green Road, is mostly in Hornchurch parish and the Hornchurch-Romford boundary ran along Brentwood Road and part of Squirrels Heath Lane. The Great Eastern Railway works provided much employment locally.

Looking south towards the Drill Inn, c.1911. Brentwood Road is directly ahead and Heath Park Road is on the right. Whatever it was that the men outside the pub were meant to be doing has been abandoned as they look towards the camera. The Drill pub itself was just inside Romford parish on what is now a roundabout where five roads converge.

Recently built housing on Abbs Cross Lane, *c.*1906. The lane ran south from Hornchurch Road, opposite what was from the 1870s the entrance to Grey Towers. It was Aspiscrosse in 1514 and is associated with the family of Le Aps who lived on Pell Street (the old name for Hornchurch High Street) in the thirteenth and fourteenth centuries.

Left: Ford Lodge, *c.*1900. This house, built or restored by Christopher Tyler around 1750, replaced an earlier house of ancient origins. It stood in Ford Lane near to where the pavilion now stands in Brittons Park.

Opposite below: The occasion is unknown but the dress suggests a date before 1910 and the venue may well be Suttons Farm. Everyone seems to be wearing their Sunday best and this may be a church outing or a treat for poorer families.

Scout or Guide camp at Grey Towers, August 1923. While the Sportsman's Battalion and New Zealand contingent were at Grey Towers the boys of the Hornchurch Section of the 3rd and 6th Romford Scout Troops acted as orderlies and messengers there. Servicemen from the camps also played a prominent part in the troops' activities from 1917 onwards, including providing Scoutmasters.

Harrow Lodge in the early 1930s. It was built in 1787 and the avenue by which the house was approached now forms the main route into Harrow Lodge Park. The house, which was damaged by fire in 1858 and by a flying bomb in 1944, was bought by Hornchurch UDC, which used it as a public library from 1936 to 1967.

Hornchurch Cottage Homes, c.1908. The Shoreditch Board of Guardians bought the eighty-six-acre Harrow Lodge Farm from Edward Dawson in 1886. They developed four acres as a self-contained village and kept twenty or so acres as a market garden, leasing the rest to a local farmer. The Cottage Homes opened in 1889 and continued as a children's home for almost a century, closing in 1984.

The Harrow on Hornchurch Road in the 1930s. This pub replaced an old thatched country hostelry pulled down in 1894 when a Mrs Dodd was the publican. It was a popular stopping place for travellers and for wagons making their way to and from the London produce markets.

Hornchurch swimming pool, Harrow Lodge Park, pictured a few years after it was opened in 1956 at a cost of £160,000. The Hornchurch District Council declared it to be 'a swimming pool of which any local authority might well feel proud; for it is undoubtedly one of the most modern and well equipped in the country.'

Park Lane in the 1930s. Although usually regarded as Romford, the area north of the hamlet of Haveringwell between Brentwood Road and Hornchurch Road was in Hornchurch parish. It was one of the first areas of the parish to be developed from the 1860s and the setting up of the Roneo office machinery factory from 1907 provided welcome employment locally.

The interior of the temporary church of Holy Cross in the early 1920s. The expansion of Hornchurch's population placed too much pressure on St Andrew's and the community between Hornchurch and Romford did not have a local church. A site at the junction of Malvern Road and Park Lane was bought for £200 and a hut was relocated from Grey Towers Camp. It was first used for services in March 1920 and became known as Holy Cross Church in 1923.

Souvenir commemorating the establishment of the temporary Holy Cross Church, 19 October 1922. This date seems to be linked to buying out the interests of the Church Army, which initially shared the premises. The Revd Charles Steer MA was the vicar of Hornchurch and the Revd Frederick Shippam was the curate-in-charge from 1921 until the parish of Holy Cross was formally established in its own right on 24 July 1925. The permanent church was built at the junction of Park Lane and Hornchurch Road in 1932 and consecrated by the Bishop of Chelmsford on 16 September 1933.

Other local titles published by Tempus

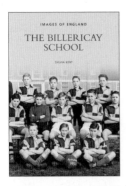

The Billericay School
SYLVIA KENT

Billericay School was created in May 1937 with only 400 pupils. With photographs of students, teachers and events, this book chronicles the sweeping changes in the school's history, including its 1968 switch to comprehensive education. The stars of the book are the students and staff. They are shown at work and at leisure, casually photographed and in posed groups, at school and on trips.
0 7524 3083 1

Harwich and Dovercourt
JOHN MOWLE

Over 200 photographs illustrate a century of history in Harwich, Dovercourt and surrounding villages such as Mistley, Parkeston, Ramsey and Little and Great Oakley. From early views of The Duke of Northumberland lifeboat in 1860 and the windmill at Ramsey in around 1930, to snapshots of Kings Quay Street in the early 1950s and Prince George's visit to Harwich in 1924, each unique picture provides an insight into a previous way of life.
0 7524 3084 X

Great Eastern Railway
GAVIN SMITH

The GER grew from bankruptcy to one of the greatest of all passenger-carrying lines. It ranged from London and the eastern suburbs, through the gentle countryside of East Anglia, to the coasts of Essex, Suffolk and Norfolk. At one time, it built the most powerful steam locomotive in the world, later it operated the most intensive steam service, now 170 photographs recall the GER's best moments.
0 7524 0639 6

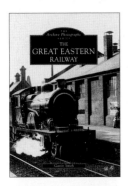

Colchester United FC 1991/92 A Season to Remember
JEFF WHITEHEAD & MATT HUDSON

Having attained its Football League status in 1950, it wasn't until over twenty years later that Colchester United FC made inspiring football history when it beat the top England team of Leeds in 1971. Thirty-nine years on from its membership gain, the team yet again hit trouble, finishing bottom of the old Fourth Division. This book charts the troubles faced by the team in 1991 and '92, and all they overcame.
0 7524 2712 1

If you are interested in purchasing other books published by Tempus, or in case you have difficulty finding any Tempus books in your local bookshop, you can also place orders directly through our website

www.tempus-publishing.com

or from **BOOKPOST**, Freepost, PO Box 29, Douglas, Isle of Man, IM99 1BQ
tel 01624 836000   email bookshop@enterprise.net